Journeys Through Prairie and Forest

Poetic Essays On the Big Questions of Life

Volume 1 — Fruits of the Spirit

Journeys Through Prairie and Forest

Poetic Essays On the Big Questions of Life

Volume 1 — Fruits of the Spirit

Volume One of a Seven-Volume Set

By Paul W. Syltie

Also by Paul W. Syltie

The Syltie Family in America

The New Eden: Millennial Agriculture,
a Key to Understanding the Kingdom of God

How Soils Work: a Study Into the God-Plane
Mutualism of Soils and Crops

Understanding God's Government,
With Contrasts to Satan's Governmental System

The Three Edens, the Story of God's Universe, Earth,
and Mankind in Conflict With the Adversary

Pathways to Joy in Marriage;
Live This Way and Happiness Will Pursue You!

The Bridge to Eden, the Arduous Passage
From This Age of Chaos to the Next Age of Perfection

Journeys Through Prairie and Forest
Volume 1. Fruits of the Spirit
by Paul W. Syltie

Publisher: IngramSpark
Editor: Paul Syltie
Editorial Assistant/Proofreader: Sandy Syltie
Photographer: Paul Syltie
Interior Design/Composition: Greg Smith
Cover Design: Greg Smith

ISBN-978-0-9980254-0-7

Printed in the United States of America

To my wonderful wife of 51 years,
and to our children and grandchildren who are the hope of the future.

Table of CONTENTS Volume 1

All photos have been taken by the author over many years.

PREFACE

WHO AM I?
WHY AM I HERE?
WHAT IS MY DESTINY?

These three questions have haunted the lives of virtually every thinking person on earth to one degree or another. They point to the very heart of our existence, and to our ultimate value, our worthiness to exist. Are we products of evolution from a primordial sea-soup, without any defined purpose in being here, or are we creations in the image of a Creator whose plan for us transcends our understanding?

The answers to these simple but profound questions dictate our decisions day by day, and ultimately the course of our careers, our friendships, our marriage partners, and how we interact within our families and communities. In many ways these answers direct our career pathway through life, and most assuredly influence our joy and fulfillment in everyday living.

I am stepping out by claiming that I have found answers — sound answers — to all three of these questions, and I am audacious enough to suggest that they are correct answers. They agree with what I understand is Truth, which is rooted in the great eternal God who made all things, and who sustains all things through the Word of His power and revelation.

But there the simplicity ends. My audacity has led to great conflicts with the realities of a corrupted earth and universe … a corrupted human race that clings to existence day-by-day upon the whims of weather and cooperation … neither of which often prosper to any race's benefit. We are always only weeks away from famine upon an earth that so often insults the farmer and gardener with drought, floods, heat, frost, or tempest.

As a farm boy raised close to nature, I have been so often forced from my peaceful home into the prairies and forests, the lakes, streams, and oceans of this wide earth to regain my bearings, to restore hope and gratitude, and to reset the pathway ahead when darkness threatens to overwhelm me. To leave the sterile unease of concrete jungles and flee to the forests and prairies of sanity has become a habit over the years — an addiction, one might say — and with that flight has emerged a continued stream of verbal expression that has leaped from my fingers. I cannot explain why, just that I must do it.

So … here is a collection of some of those writings expounded over the years, some of them clearly poetic, and some of them bordering more on short essays. I attempted some way to categorize them to make them flow, but they have defied clear organization; each item is too complex to easily arrange in a coherent order. Thus, I have let them fall where they may within broad categories, and have applied pictures I have taken through the years to emphasize the messages. Photographing nature has been a passion much of my life; these images speak louder and more eloquently than my words.

I hope you enjoy these messages, and are brought into a closer association with the Creator as a result so you will be able to answer these three big questions a bit better yourself. Let us walk together through the prairies and forests of our land, our beautiful, God-given land that speaks to us so eloquently if we will but open our ears and listen.

PREAMBLE

How do we understand the human mind in all of its incredible intricacies, that science has only begun to comprehend? Add to that the human spirit, which heaps an infinitely greater dimension to the matter. This is the stuff we are dealing with in these verses — beauty, peace, joy, patience, worth — those matters that matter most to us but which we seem to understand the least ... at least within this world of deception, war, and frayed nerves.

We must begin where the mind and spirit begin, where beauty and fulfillment find their expression, where the neurons interface with the unseen spirit world to grant us speech and imagination, creativity and kindness, and everything else worth living for.

We must turn around those negative emotions of jealousy, anger, hatred, and depression and replace them with the joy, peace, humility, kindness, and patience that mesh much better with the human spirit. These ways of the spirit are not for our destruction, but for our uplift every day.

Measuring Beauty

I try to understand what beauty is,
 And have resolved that it is of the individual who respects it,
Who sees it and knows it — from every nation and tongue —
 And no formula on earth or in heaven exists to quantify it ...
Except for the qualities placed within it to make it shine in righteousness,
 Be it of the human, animal, bird, fish, reptile, or plant world:

　　Joy, love, kindness, hope, faith, gentleness, humility, patience, goodness, and the like.

Whatever expresses these things — in one's face, a leaf, a flower, a deer, or a bird — we know as beauty,
And dimensions and design take second place.

Those Modern "Heresies"

Jealousy is good ... if it be toward one's wife and children, and to the Creator of all;
 Anger is good ... if it be toward evil and the vile works of men;
Hate is good ... if it be against lawlessness, corruption, and disobedience to holy commands;
 Depression is good ... if it direct one closer to his Creator, to humility and love.

Enthusiasm

Children awakening, wide-eyed and ready …
  To fish for the big ones,
  To cast in the line and wait for the tug;
Young chicks furiously crowding toward the open door in morning's reds and
  yellows …
  Half flying, half running out the gate,
  Peeping, searching expectantly for grasshoppers and elusive beetles;
Grandfathers, old and sage of life's mysteries …
  Greeting running children with open arms,
  Eyes keen and limbs yet nimble, tasting the wisdom of elders' years,
  ever mindful of sunset's last rays;
Young men and women heeding the call to succeed
  Before energies flag, and children flee the nest,
  While day is yet young, when hearts beat warm and fast
  to challenges priceless.

Capetown, South Africa. *Who can quell the enthusiasm of young kids from any nation who are out on a hike? This enthusiasm ought to infect every facet of our lives from sunup to sundown.*

Faith, Not Sight

Thrust within this warp in time I fly at breakneck pace
    Along the unseen way of life, towards ways unveiled to face
My master's paintings—finished art of beauty, grief, and sweat—
    Tomorrow's scenes complete and full, but I can't see them yet.

Defense

A war you are in, fierce battle in array,
    So forget not your defense 'mid life's cruel fray,
Lest haply your fare deals harsh wounds not a few,
    But rather prepare lusty bulwarks around you …
That Satan's sharp forays not strike his cruel death,
    As faith, hope, and charity grace soul and flesh.

The Cure

Born to live forever, yet death stares pensively
    At every flesh-born servant who lives faithfully…
Despite concerted efforts to hold the beast at bay,
    Death's ever-present sorrows return to spoil the day.
I am not prone to query how God has formed this clay.
    His plan is just and perfect, for Adam's sin must pay
The price amongst us sons of men, a hefty one for sure.
    But with my death I pray His love will deftly find a cure.

Yellowstone Park, Wyoming.
The unfailing eruptions of Old Faithful geyser every 45 to 125 minutes in Yellowstone Park remind us all of the need to be faithful in all of our relationships and responsibilities, especially to our Creator.

Chapter 3

Forgiveness

Forgive

Frustrated with error, forsaken of rest,
    In anguish and torment we suffer the test,
That others in anger not cast us away
    When we miss the mark, and with humble heart say...
"Forgive me!"

Forgiveness

Thrust amongst the sea of men this soul in deep travail
    Seeks the joy of plenteous feasts along life's boisterous trail,
Seeing how the best of friendships often disappoint
    The best of dreams, the highest hopes which God's desires anoint.
Oh, grant me flight from bitterness, to shun such deviance,
    And let the path of true forgiveness light with brilliance.

Johannesburg, South Africa. *The closeness that a zebra family displays in its frequent huddles in the savanna reminds us of the need to grow closer to our neighbors and forgive them of their trespasses against us.*

Forgiveness

Treasure Forgiveness

Forgiveness, that vivifying infinitude, piercing each fiber of innocent mind,
   Releasing trouble's grip from harlotry's bosom, opening vistas of clear,
   blossoming fields,

Fragrant and swaying before springtime's fresh, pure south winds,
   Holding peace as her fellow kinsman, joy as a healthy companion,
   love and humility as true friends.

Release the grip of harsh anger and insult:
   "Revel in my light load," resounds forgiveness,

That boundless treasure reserved for the broken-hearted.

Forgiveness in Marriage

A marriage without forgiveness cannot a night endure,
   For darkness would enshroud it, and dash it's precepts pure,

To nether worlds unspoken, life's emptiness unfurled,
   For two hearts can't unite unless the self to hell be hurled.

I donned the robe of love today, to lure my wife so fair
   Amongst the verdant hillsides, the fragrant blossoms there

Erasing debts of sadness, the tide of schemes gone wrong.
   Oh, let us vaunt forgiveness, its sunshine be our song!

Fredericksburg, Texas. *Nature preaches continually the mantra of forgiveness,
   even in a dry and thirsty land where the brutal drought of a semi-arid climate
   is greeted with the awesome wonder of bluebonnets shouting forth reprieve
   from nature's harsh blows dealt to the earth and its residents.*

An Endless Hope

We reach forth in hope despite the chaos of worlds of desperation on all sides,
 Recalling always that our fortress lies not in flesh and blood's impotent sword,
But in the power and might of the Eternal Living God, who loves us dearly,
 And scatters from us the horrors of evil that threaten to overwhelm us.

Descent of Man

I looked at the seat of power and expected perfection,
 But found error shot through the halls of leadership.
The courts of the world must show forth justice, I considered …
 But lo, false witnesses echoed forth their cry, and bribes rent justice asunder.
Surely the homes of the righteous would yield hope of life's innermost joys,
 But even the seat of society's power proved fractured and depraved,
 bereft of strength and love.
The focus of spiritual power must certainly deliver righteous expectations
 to wandering wayfarers upon the earth,
But even there error beset every turn, doctrines incomplete and perverse,
 evil tainting what ought be pure.

Continued on page 10

Sinai, South Dakota. *Thousands upon thousands of Canadian geese stream overhead toward southern climes, in the hope of surviving the assaults of winter as the cold and snow make life untenable in the North.*

Hope

Continued from page 9

So life began to be drudgery, a great burden that I could not verbalize
through this inadequate language,
And I pined away in grief, wondering how existence might have meaning
during these few, short days on the earth.
The injustices of my fellow man I could not change, so obvious they seemed,
Though I too clung to error unseen of myself.
Then where lay purpose and meaning in life, where I could hope to find
the love I sought so earnestly amidst grief at this world's table?
Looking up I saw my Father, in loving kindness reaching out to me in my anguish,
Soothing my wounds of soul, placating the heartache burning within my breast,
Speaking kind words to me, heard only by the birds and the creatures
that lay in silent anticipation all around me
As raindrops sparkled on the deep-green mat of grass around,
caressing my tear-stained face,
Breathing new life — new truth — into weary bones.

Hope in Weakness

When bodies lie low, and hopes grow dim,
Then the Eternal will rise up strong,
Pushing down bulwarks that stand before Him,
Pleading your cause, righting all wrong.

Hope of the Saints

"Be ye perfect", resounds the royal degree,
   Upon the sea of imperfection,
Men's hearts yearning to be set free
   From the thralldom of error and corruption.

Yet in peace we reside, knowing well no perfect sight
   May possibly rest before us in worlds of decay,
But in due course all error shall be made right,
   When in the Kingdom our bodies free of sin …

   Shall ride free as the ocean waves
   Upon a glassy emerald sea.

Imperfection

When to myself this eye doth see,
   Imperfection covers me.
Like cloaks of darkness 'midst the light,
   Tis the error dims my sight.
Yet onward must this sojourn sail,
   Through forest, prairie, hill, and vale,
Accepting something less than whole
   Within this flesh and blood and soul;
That though I cringe to miss the mark,
   Fine treasures wait for those who hark
To joyous paths repentance brings,
   The Kingdom's hope forever sings.

Hope's Revival

There once was hope,
   But the blind man picked it off the tree,
And it fell and rotted over the months,
   To become soil for a dozen more lively trees,
Planted by the fertile, supple rivers of time.

Hope

Wisdom and Hope

I seek to create wisdom, but find it is already of old.
   The present and future are but mirrors of the past,
And nothing is new under the sun.
   In my vanity the mind seeks to vaunt itself,
Yet it is thrown down, broken asunder, its wisdom turned backwards.
   I ask for wisdom, and it is given.
Lessons of life and their portent are explored and revealed,
   stored as honey for the future.
Yet, all of this hope for self-endearment evaporates alongside
   the ways of the Creator.
Man is so small, so weak, so insignificant.
   In one moment his life can be snuffed out.
But God is eternal and omnipotent, the Creator and King of all.
   So well did the patriarchs of old know such truth,
   and even now await the fruit of their hope.
Will there be an end to all of these trials upon the earth?
   No, not until God erases one's physical existence, or until He literally comes;
   only then will one's painful physical trials cease.
All the while I abhor myself for the deceit and inconsistencies in my nature,
   which of itself knows no perfection, and knows no truth.
So I will await patiently for that great day in the future, the fruit of all hope
   from now to eternity.

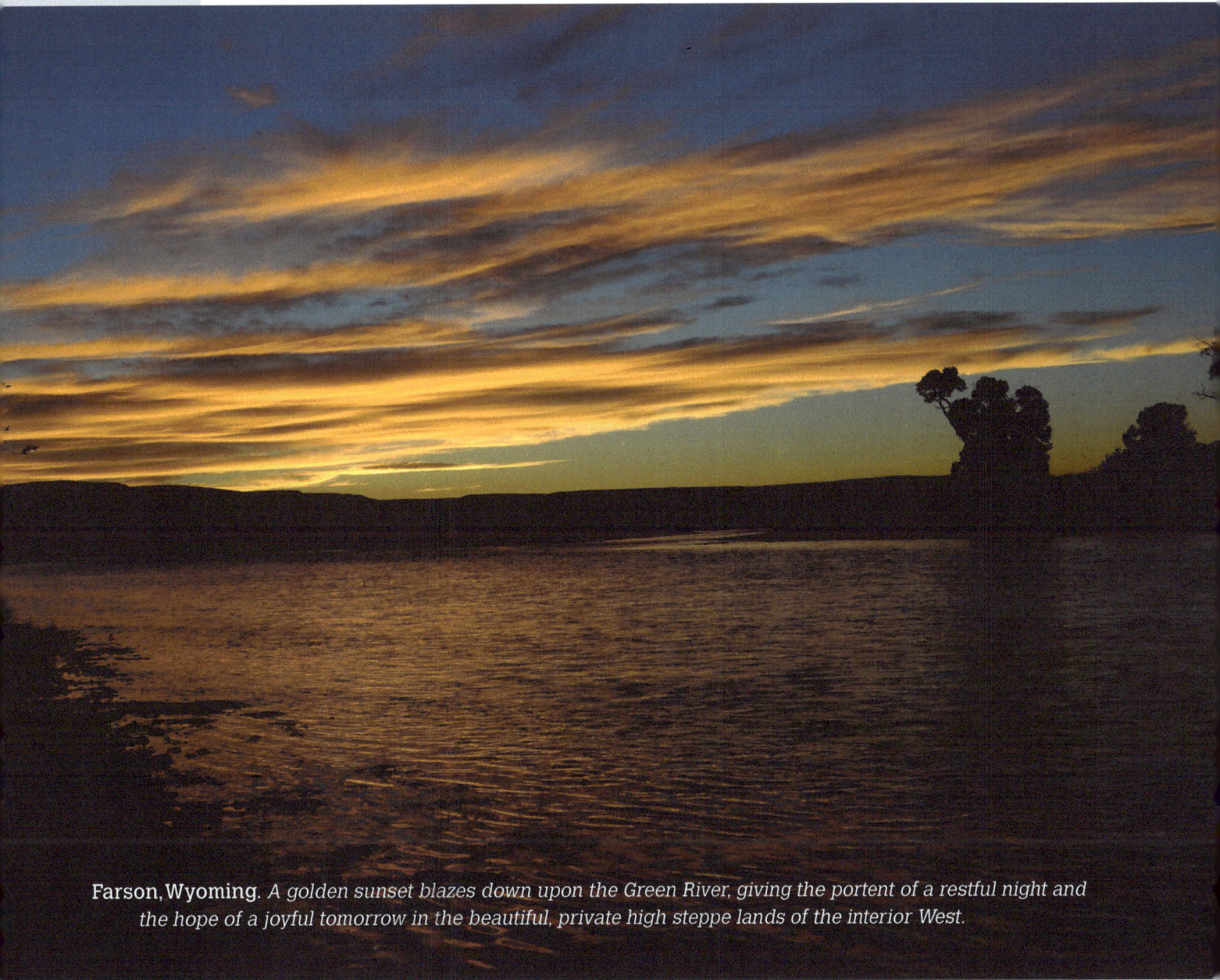

Farson, Wyoming. *A golden sunset blazes down upon the Green River, giving the portent of a restful night and the hope of a joyful tomorrow in the beautiful, private high steppe lands of the interior West.*

Double Cabin, Wyoming. *Bluebells droop down as if bowing in silent reverence in the crystal clear air of the Absaroka Mountains. Might we also take on this humility as we bow to the Creator of all that is?*

The Fallen Fruitful

Chapter 5

The fruitful tree, sprouting blossoms plentifully throughout
    Rested consternated on its side, its branches stout,
Arrayed to hold it firmly situated on the ground,
    Roots a-glare, the windy storm to earth this tree did pound.

Yet fruitful did this soldier of the forest quite remain,
    Amidst the taller splendor of the forest's vast domain,
For year by year the fallen friend of men and bird and kine
    Blossomed forth in splendid fare despite its humble clime.

This fallen tree — my friend, my kin — delights my daily dream
    Through deep-green forest, shaded thicket, meditation's stream,
For I myself have fallen from my perch of grasping pride,
    And rest braced firmly in God's soil, limbs fruitful, self denied.

Aukland, New Zealand. *Dried fronds of sea grass overlook the Tasman Sea, bowing to the sea breezes that grace the North Island, in humble submission to the elements of the ocean climate.*

Chapter 6

Joy

Fulfillment

Enjoyment in life is doing what you enjoy,
 Seeing tangible fruits of your labors in earthly realms.
Of utmost fulfillment is the intangible,
 Life abundant spread abroad by your light,
Planting seeds of increase throughout this darkened world
 Wherever your footsteps lead …
A Johnny Appleseed of the spirit,
 Illuminating temporal vistas through joy of heart.

Riches, But No Pleasure

So fickle a notion that men seek today:
 Gain riches aplenty but health throw away.
What good is the gold when the spark of life fails,
 And fortunes lie idle as aching soul wails …

"Today I am tired, I shall not adventure
 To gain hold of nature's expoundable pleasure;
Though mountain peaks beckon me come to their feast,
 Yet reach them I can't, though my gold be increased."

Seek joy in life when your heart is yet tender.
 Roam fragrant forests and beauty engender,
But keep healthful vistas until death's dim trigger;
 What gain is great riches if years yield no vigor?

Johannesburg, South Africa. *A gnu rejoices by kicking up its heels in the fresh, clean air of the southern Africa savanna. We can also experience the joy in living by seeking the fruits of the spirit within the created world.*

Well-Being

So strange the ways of mind and spirit, wending out their plan,
  When body aches and suffering breaks the heart of striving man.
Then enters softly humbling joy, so deftly through the pain,
  Sore wounds to bind and health restore, Raphekah's wealth to gain.

Pritchett, Texas. *Freshly unfolding grape leaves curl and
expand as millions of tiny cells multiply and expand into the form
the Creator designed for them, gracing the earth in joyful praise
of the refurbished earth.*

Nature Unfolding

Nestled within nature's limbs, stretched among her deep shadows,
glistening, warming sunbeams …

I rest on rocks weather-beaten, lichen-covered — orange, gray, brown —
cracked and craggy,

Split asunder by trailing, gnarled, beautiful roots;
Pines aspiring ever upwards, gently swaying amidst fall breezes …

Whispering joys untold, unfolding dreams too deep to fathom,
Lessons innate in greens, browns, rusty yellows, drifting piney scents
through warming canopies of love,

Shrouding blistering summer sun's tirade amidst cooling shade upon her feet
of green gold,

Beauty ever blanketing the lost laurels of earthly hidden battles,
Ever consuming defeat with victory, moiling desperate chaos into serene order …
lasting forever …

Seed heads, flowers, browning pliant blades of Black Hills grasses ever swaying
resiliently to caressing breezes,

Ever melding hope with the lost strife of befuddled men,
Confounding man's wisdom, challenging his disclaimed sanity with lessons
too deep to fathom,

Yielding tears to war-torn eyes awestruck among scenes too humble and strong
to describe, much less perceive …

Opening vistas never before conceived, vistas of faith and power, might and joy,
character within the creation's glorious majesty unending.

Alberta, Canada. *The stuff of life! A farmer rejoices in the beauty of a life-giving soil that he has
nurtured over many years to be full of organic matter and fertility for the growth of abundant,
nutritious crops for the sustenance of mankind.*

Chapter 7

Kindness

Kindness to Enemies

Condemn not your adversary,
 But walk in his shoes a little while,
For he knows not what he does,
 A soldier of fate cast upon the earth
In ignorance and want,
 Flailing aimlessly amidst the fiery darts
He cannot understand,
 Casting them back at you in confusion,
And fear of loneliness, failure, defeat.
 A day will come when he too
Shall beam upon the face of his Creator
 And see himself ... much differently,
In clarity of who he is.

Bryce Canyon National Park, Utah. *Even ground squirrels and other animals express kindness to one another in ways us humans ought to every day. Affection for one another brings out the best in each of us, and should never be left for others to initiate.*

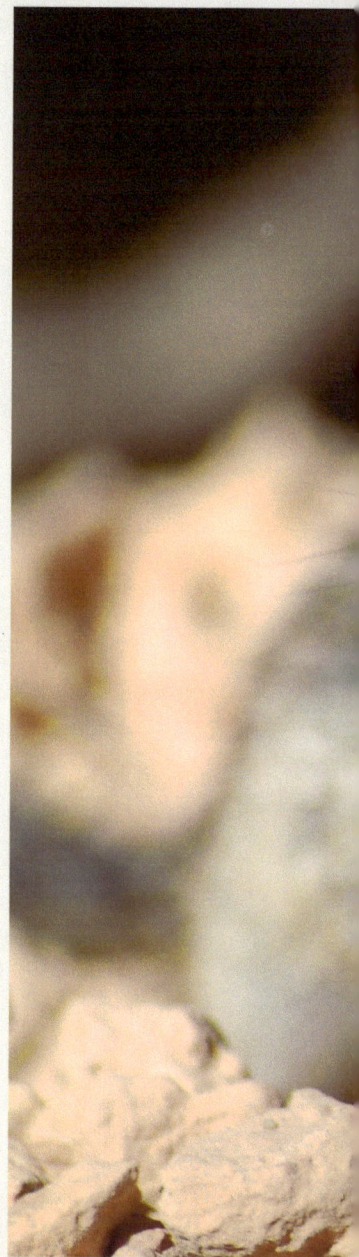

Liberty

Caught amidst the currents of man's ignoble social schemes
  The son of heaven's calling finds his life a newborn dream,
Wrested from the fearsome clutches of earth's leadership,
  Suddenly a freeborn man, untied from mankind's grip.

His liberty sends waves of joy through every field and garden,
  Of his new life in spirit's plane, the fear of men discarded,
And now he grasps his liberty in serving with his gifts,
  Those others who in former days might grasp him in their grip.

Men were not designed to rule o'er others in God's plan,
  But serve them with those wondrous gifts throughout his whole lifespan.
And when this truth should show itself across all tribes and nations,
  All wars and conflicts — big and small — shall bask in glad cessation.

Galapagos Islands, Ecuador. *As a pelican soars above the crashing waves of a Galapagos seashore, so the liberty that ought to be upon the conscience of every one of us should propel us towards the freedom of spirit that is inherent within a mind captured to the spirit of the Creator.*

Love

Bits and Pieces

Bits and pieces do I find
Of love amidst this world of mine,
Fraught with darkness 'round each turn,
Lost, unable to discern
The ways that bring us joy and peace …
A world of souls in pain increase.
Oh, how I long for days ahead
When in the morn I leave my bed
Rejoicing with the singing lark,
Footpaths lit among the dark
And grievous roads we all must shed,
That I with bits and pieces tread.

Essence of Love

These hands, this mind, these lips of golden words, yet hardly spoken,
Give birth to poised realities, the germ of cocoons broken.
Fair cities rise from faceless plains, DaVinciesque the paintings,
Machines adroitly engineered, the farmer's hard-fought plantings.
Yet should these hands, this mind, these lips invent man's greatest thrall,
They would as one fall to the ground as worthless gifts to all,
Unless within their essence lies the boundless gift of love,
No good shall rise, no blessing thrive from all of what men does.

Pritchett, Texas. *A white iris with its incredibly complex and gorgeous array of yellows and foldings virtually engulfs the spirit, inviting one's entrance into its fragrant interior of heavenly scents and awesome expression of creative love.*

Lifting Brothers

Oh, that men would strive to lift their brothers from the pit,
    Instead of trampling on their backs in search of long-lost worth.
How joyous would this world become — man's cruel offenses quit,
    If but the simple acts of love upon each soul would berth.

Love in All Eons

Love, that self-redeeming character of being,
    Impresses forever her wit within men's hearts,
Streams forth its predestined selfless joy,
    Enrapturing all that is, binding faith and hope,
Encapsulating the fullness of the I AM …
    Our past, our present, our future purpose of being
Throughout the eons.

Johannesburg, South Africa. *Though grizzled and coarse, two warthogs express love to one another by a head-to-head show of affection upon the fruitful savanna of South Africa.*

Love

Love

Is it a feeling deep inside, the "heart", we say, with peace resides,
   In sensing mushy stomach pits as chemistry her potion fits?
Or does the concept deeper run than reaping folly, fun or pun,
   And wind its tendrils well within the total stuff of man and kin?

What does love say, let's hear her plea, lest should from sanity one flee.
   Does man know best to serve his fare upon this earth his wealth to spare?
Or can it be his gelt runs short when to himself vain truth resorts?
   Yes, truth leads wisely to all sense, so let love speak, let truth commence.

"I know your ways, small men of earth, but yet with hope I spend my worth,
   While straining strongly at your bits to wipe the coldness from your wits.
You wish to hold me close, but then reject my face now and again
   That surely one might think I'd flee; but wait my master — I serve thee!

"The missiles lurch and clatter forth from underground encasements north;
   The rumbling tanks and cracking guns tear viciously my mother's sons,
While soldiers ask amid the din of cannon and distorted grin,
   'What sense lies here inside this trench?' I answer not; such hate to quench.

Continued on page 32

Sinai, South Dakota. *Any farm boy of the Midwest who has bent down and smelled the heavenly aroma of a wild rose knows how inexpressibly delightful is this dazzling flower of the Plains of North America. The experience is the epitome of love expressed by a Creator who made the creation so good and uplifting for the residents of the earth.*

Continued from page 30

"Yet elsewhere stands a man so tall his visage overshadows all
   Small men who spit and slap his form, for want of error to reform;
Since hate springs forth when some be forced from my pure ways to lesser course.
   He speaks my name, he minds my ways, yet faggots burn and end his days.

"Or yonder lies a grave where my pure ways meant death when one wife cried
   To warn her mate of wayward minds, where darkness lurked and eyes grew blind.
He heard my call of prophets old, of giving life for friends so bold,
   Whose sole end was to follow my Creator though the bullets fly.

"I strive to give what's good in me to save men from the churning sea,
   Where this world's masses blindly swim downstream so swiftly, down the grim
And toilsome, brooding sin-sick ways of hate's shrewd master, his great sway
   Unfolding waves of searing pain, black misery and pointless aim.

"If men would seek my wealthy way, he'd walk with joyful songs each day.
   His way would speak of pride rung short for sake of reading my report,
And searching for the pleasant word, a helping hand, a means to gird
   Your neighbors with the goodness you would likewise wish him to you do.

"My way is kindly, gentle, meek, it strives for reason, never seeks
   To vaunt the self or fill with pride the ego within which resides
So many roots of wrath and strife which rips compassion (my own wife)
   To shattered shreds and leaves life bare; come visit my lush pastures fair.

"You'll find no wish to hear bad words, but only good reports which serve
   To lift up men both right and left and leave them stronger for all tests.
Patience is my close-held guide. I'm never rude, I never chide;
   A beastly manner holds no sway, nor jealousy its selfish way.

Continued on page 33

"Come to my fruitful stores of grace, and others' faults please soon erase,
  For glory comes from humbling pride instead of thrusting friends aside.
Believe the best in others' lives, forgive their motes, their stubborn drives,
  And cast your own logs far aside; embrace your friend, arms open wide.

"Come meet me — LOVE — I never end; you won't be sorry, my dear friend,
  For friends we are should our paths meet and you decide to don your feet
With brighter shoes to light the way within this grievous, darkened day.
  Place me ahead of all your plans; I'll help you ease your whole life span."

Love to a Neighbor

A man of talents may his trade perfect a thousand times,
  But if he fails in loving care to lift his neighbor's hopes,
Those gifts he's given may as well be cast out and forgotten,
  For selfish hearts can never raise the light of joy's tomorrow.

Reject the Machine

Man rejects the machine, he does … deep down, deep within his psyche.
  Rather, love he craves, to serve his companion in need, to search out the living,
Not mindless motion of cold, hard steel, silicon chip computations,
  Or vagaries of unfeeling robot friendships made only for a season
Amidst the warmth of hearts akin to heavenly palaces, the hearts won over
  To worlds kind and beautiful, far from the grinding monotony of beating engines.

Love
What is Love?

Attend my words of love, young boy, these words of crying love,
    Whose song rings out to all the world of men so long since dead;
And grieve for those less humbly swayed, on pride's road high above,
    The fall from which destroys strong men; return to love instead.

"But what is love?" one voice rang out, its tone as distant cries,
    Which barely rose above the din of earthquakes, bombs, and shouts
Of passersby who glibly viewed dank streets with bloodshot eyes,
    And bowed their knees on concrete grime to cities tall or stout.

The answer came in lurching blurts above the roiling mass,
    Of autos, trucks, huge factories, jet planes and men's hot breath.
"What? Love? Oh, yes, that long-lost word. Oh, surely you won't press
    Us men of perfect wisdom to pursue this to the death.

"Why our own institutions with great minds so far refined,
    Above the dismal whims of slaves below our plateau here
Cannot be judged for truth, for truth indeed we do define;
    To question love, how dare you, boy!" the voice said with a sneer.

"And furthermore," the voice rang out, "love's object is all self.
    It needn't touch your neighbor, boy, for how may he help you?
The stuff in life is building hefty bridges for yourself,
    And burning them before your brother hastens over too."

Continued on page 37

Yellowstone Park, Wyoming. *The laughing waters of a cascade in a mountain stream epitomize the loving voice of God Himself as He speaks to us while we traverse the creation, meant for rejuvenating the soul and revealing Himself to all that will look and listen.*

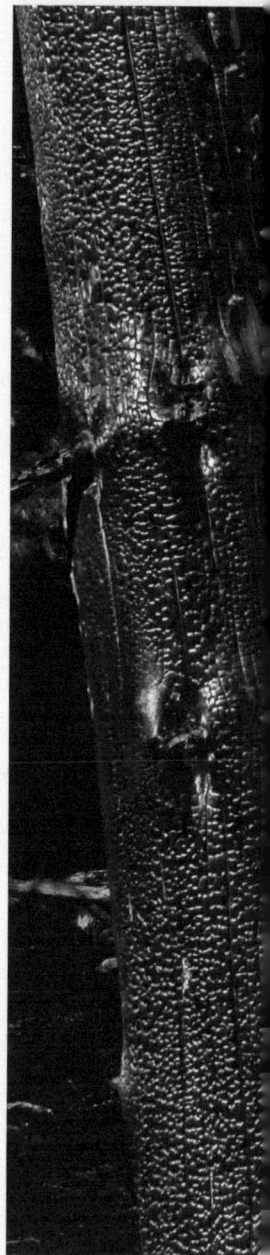

Continued from page 34

A few heads hung down to the ground, they would not turn or smile,
 But cried in silent agony while shedding precious tears.
How great this cold world could have been had selfish dreams been piled
 Upon the trash of ages past, men paralyzed by fear.

But slowly, silently the few remembered what was said
 For all learned men to know (but who'd rejected sanity),
Of hope for ages lost among the living and the dead;
 Their eyes turned upward, onward, beamed towards God's infinity.

So faith in life renewed itself, and love gained strength again.
 It sealed a pact with patience, kindness, firm resolve to do
The will of greater powers mightily averse to men,
 Those ways defined by love sublime, lost sanity renew.

Sinai, South Dakota. *The eye-popping reds and yellows of a native poppy, attended by a curious fly, shout forth the love of the Creator to all passersby. The character of love is impossible to hide.*

Where is Love?

Ideas flow fluently from the mouths of learned educators,
    steeped in the traditions of men.
Onward prate inconsolable doctrines unending, causing eyelids to droop,
    eyes to grow dim, the mind to become dull of hearing.
Cold, sterile, plain brick and concrete surround the imagination
    with unkind harshness, uncomely sameness … gray and dull browns,
While unseeing eyes pass by on streets and sidewalks, from behind countless
    steering wheels of endless belching hulks plying the pavement.

    I look up amid the choking fumes and ask, "Where is love?"

Books unending, row upon row of all sorts and sizes,
    without beginning or end,
Couch with the fertile, fetid minds of children infinitely comprehensive,
    full of hopes and dreams, homes and fields …
Yet cast asunder beneath gadgets of steel, toys for the demise
    of short-sighted ventures created for ultimate destruction;
Unable to perceive truth while the blind lead the blind, and error waxes
    mightily against truth which one day must be revealed.

    Yet the pages close, and truth is hidden … for a later day …
    and I ask, "Where is love?"

Continued on page 40

Farson, Wyoming. *How is it that an arid western land can nurture such a lovely and delicate primrose flower, whose stamens and pistil cast sharp shadows across the clear white petals of this most exquisite flower?*

9 Love

Chapter

Continued from page 39

Tender, supple, green blades of grass shove lustily against the edges
of the sidewalks, between cracks,

Where footsteps somehow forget to blacken and besmirch the earth,
failing to completely obliterate the green.

Oh, for the city to stop in its tracks, crumble into a billion tiny fragments
to yield soil fertile for generations of farms, fields, pastures … and hopes;

For the streets, superhighways, plastic and metal cans littering
the discarded land to retreat into their own bitter end;

And as I walk across the fields, grown up in weeds,
with sounds of the city at my back, I ask, "Where is love?"

Warm raindrops caress my head, shoulders, face, and hands as across the
meadow I walk, oblivious to the din of the city and her industry …
always at my back.

The twilight is fading, and the rumbling storm to the west continues its push
northeastward, granting healing powers to a crying land,

Perceived through greedy economic eyes as an exploit, another parameter,
an "it" … but my footsteps continue, and on to the west, toward the storm
I pace, thunder now cracking in a resounding chorus amid wildly
flashing lightning, and fitful, earthy breezes.

Oh, to embrace the earth, the good earth, and cling to her, become one
with her, and forget eternally the foulness of man's distorted dreary dreams,
bent upon greed and vanity.

The lightning flashes and the thunder crashes; warm, huge drops
shower down suddenly, and I look up and ask, "Where is love?"

I long to touch her, the good earth, as on a warm, sunny spring afternoon
when the soil is cold yet from winter, when the tender bluestem is
gingerly pushing through fleeing winter's brown mat.

Continued on page 41

She knows no error, no fear, nor has ever withheld compassion toward her
 fellow workers, always inviting, consoling, redeeming;
For as the Creator dressed and adorned her, fragrantly and with infinite charm,
 so the created beings of millennial promise pampered and caressed
 her produce, her forests and prairies, mountains and vales.
Rain now pelts down upon my weary crown, flowing in great streaming rivers
 to the ground, but to the west I continue to peer, straining ahead for
 glimpses of blue sky and stars studding the clearing canopy above.

 So the rain assuages and the clouds move rapidly on to the east …
 and I ask, "Where is love?"

The soil now spongy beneath the knee-high carpet of prairie grass,
 my footsteps lead onward once again for a time until the faint light of
 evening fades to the west, the skies clear, and a glorious canopy
 of brilliant stars studs the heavens above.
A serenade of crickets and frogs gently graces the cooling nighttime air,
 so clean and crisp, so invigorating and peaceful.
Waves of contentment and gratitude pass though my shaking body,
 and I drop to my knees,
And again I ask, "Where is love?" as the far-off drone of a jetliner filters
 through the placid night air.

 What care does one possess to retrieve a sobbing body from the
 soil and grass upon which it has fallen, sopping wet with fallen
 rain and torn with pretentions of better days, dreams, and devices?
 How does one unlock the stores of compassion, and tap the reservoirs of hope?

I looked up from the wet, grassy footpath and pleaded to my Maker …
 and He heard … and answered as only He can … from the deep, undying hope
 of a father who never forsakes a son: "I AM love."

JOURNEYS THROUGH PRAIRIE AND FOREST Poetic Essays On The Big Questions of Life

Why Me?

I pleaded in ignorance, "Why me?
  Why choose this soul to suffer such stormy seas,
Such raging waters to drown?
  On bended knee this slave of unseen spheres
Fights tooth and nail throughout the years,
  Foes large and small … victories amidst toilsome tears."

I knew not what I said; that I knew,
  Yet raised my cry, what could I do?
The piecing spears of martyrdom grew,
  Upon the sea of glass I tread,
Above earth's blackened, cindered dead
  While thousands greet … their Maker wed.

And again I exclaimed, "Why me?"
  The answer clearly spoke softly though the night:

"Love, dear friend, love."

And I cried once more,
  This time in joy,
Which had not left me yet.

Yellowstone Park, Wyoming. *Boiling water bursts forth from a steaming pool and breaks into a myriad of pieces … like our lives sometimes when confronted by trials impossible to resolve through ordinary means. Yet, through raging waters and violent waves we stay the course, assured that nothing will overtake us beyond our ability to endure.*

10 Patience

Dreams of Wandering

My heart wanders across meadows fair, bright and sunny, fragrant, sweet,
  While sojourning amidst concrete and steel, drone of engines, acrid city air,

In brilliant dreams of worlds unseen — realities awaiting their day.
  They shall come: just a little while, just a bit longer.

Patience will work her great works,
  And suffering need abide no longer

Among the living ... yes, the living, whose hope I seek,
  When the enemy — death — is defeated forever.

Galapagos Islands, Ecuador. *We tend to equate patience with turtles, whose slow and ponderous treks across the ground evoke the element of patience to our thoughts, though surely in a tortoise's mind they are by no means slowing the pace!*

Peace & Contentment

Captive of Light

Nothing in this world of men so blind
   Contorts his fickle gods as peace of mind.
Beset by mass confusion on each side
   The lost lead countless lost to death beside
Such quiet waters just beyond their reach,
   A chasm firmly planted for to teach
The simple ways of law and love that show
   How darkness of the blind may cease to grow,
Amongst the thorns and nettles harsh and cruel
   Along the easy road to selfdom's school.
Become a captive journeyman to Light,
   And minds of peace your hope they shall delight.

Contentment

Contentment, that joyful roll of security
   You will never reach by striving;
A gift it is to those relieved
   Of conscience's bitter accusations
At days' end … a gift to the pure of heart.

Pritchett, Texas. *Perfect peace: a mother and her firstborn child sitting among the trees of the east Texas forest, wondering what this little life might bring to the world wherein peace seems to find few places to rest.*

Peace & Contentment

Peace Amongst Cottonwoods

Here amidst the cottonwoods, stream a-bubbling by,
    My family rests securely set beneath the azure sky,
Without a fear of life's grim horror's fraught through lives of many,
    This lone clan of God's great love shall thrive amidst His plenty.

For a few resourceful days sequestered 'neath His wings,
    We shall run freely through His meadows while our spirit sings
Of worlds far-flung from this creation fraught with death and pain,
    This next eon of beauty, joy, enraptured not in vain,
When all His seed shall shout for joy to greet the rising sun,
    As surely as the seasons pass, that day His Kingdom come.

Rest

Rest, oh weary soul, rest
    From summer's torrid heat and vanquished goals.
Rest from Babylon's careless blunders
    Cast before you as stumbling blocks,
Which you did not seek nor hold dear.
    Let burning sands of blighted summer
Lose their grip amidst dreams of worlds beyond,
    That new abode where loss of hope
Can never find its resting place,
    And weary souls that in this world cannot abide
Shall find their solace forever draped
    In awesome dreams of worlds to come.

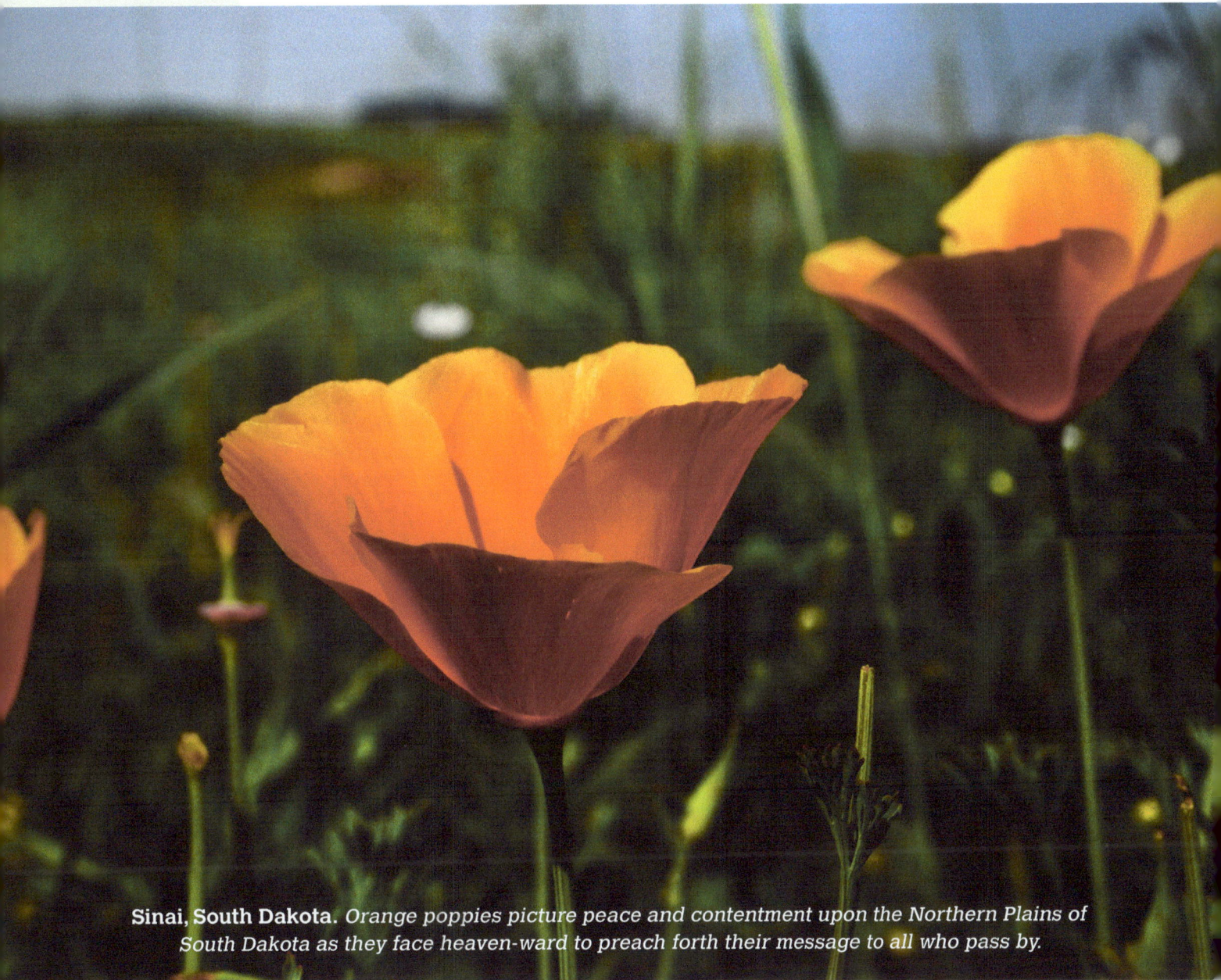

Sinai, South Dakota. *Orange poppies picture peace and contentment upon the Northern Plains of South Dakota as they face heaven-ward to preach forth their message to all who pass by.*

Peace & Contentment

Simple Peace

Simple peace …

Sitting atop boulders reaching toward heaven,
Doves cooing distantly, mournfully as fresh westerly breezes briskly cool my aching limbs;
Shadows lengthening along the velvety, sinuous slopes, great heaps slung
   with infinite variety toward the depths of ravines,
Meshing silently along the march toward the sea from fading evening sunset slopes.

Simple peace …

Junipers and sagebrush, bunchgrass and desert flowers nestled among rocks and flowing slopes,
Clinging tenaciously against raging storms, torrid summer sun, and smothering snow;
Lofty pines clustering atop windswept mountain peaks, along northern foothill shoulders,
   sheltered from summer's heat.

Simple peace …

Twittering mountain bluebirds, so brilliant and deft, proudly defending their domain;
Cottontails unafraid, no harshness even shown, for seldom has man startled their curiosity;
Buzzing, crackling grasshoppers, brown as the rocks, unseen among the pebbles and grass,
   sheltered among the helter-skelter cascade of browns and grays of scattered
   rocks and pebbles, crowned with brilliant orange and deep green lichens.

Continued on page 53

Alaska. *Standing in array, three horses exude well-fed contentment, their cares well in tow
   even after the harsh Alaskan winter has passed.*

Pritchett, Texas. *Standing in stark contrast to the white, billowing thunderhead beyond, the skeleton of a tree decrees the realities of a harsh life upon the earth, but with that reality the plain message of resignation to the fate of all life in this age of decay brought on by Adam's fall from perfection.*

Continued from page 51

Peace & Contentment

Simple peace …

Plunging hillsides where few men tread, where money lays few claims for exploit …
thus few lie the footprints upon this hallowed earth.

Here I lay me down and rest, none to disturb me,

While the Eternal consoles my spirit, breathing life where death once lurked,
shielding me from the storms of prairies and woodlands …
here on this desert of hope and reprieve, here on this island of secluded meditation;

For hearts of the lost lie elsewhere and cannot find repose amid such self-revealing calm.

Simple peace …

Indeed, I am not alone,
For the Eternal is here beside me,

And never shall I stumble from this glorious view, this wonderful plan
set wondrously clear before me.

What I Seek

I have nothing in this world …
Yet I have everything.

It is eternal prosperity I seek,
Not temporal pleasures which vanish like the wind.

Peace and contentment grace my abode,
While worlds around me collapse in agony.

I am content with enough,
And seek not luxury.

The impossible I accomplished, never flinching,
Tossing failure away as dross,

Never in vain glory, never claiming victory of myself,
But casting full glory upon the One who gave me life.

12 Persistence

Persistence

Tired, depleted, looking for rest,
    Ever achieving, fulfilling the test,
In spite of great odds that cast the heart down,
    Moving yet upward, defying the ground.

So my heart whispers, foretelling the ends
    Of each precious exploit our faithful God sends,
Onward to heaven's gate, so soars my soul
    Always in prayer … rehearsing the goal.

Oh let heavy eyelids forever remain
    Open and vibrant despite the heart's pain;
Let vivid visions of joy leap within
    A soul fraught with triumph, keen hopes never dim.

Persistence, It Grows

Gazing toward the elms and willows, bare above the snow,
    Bathed in smiling winter's sun, afresh with morning's glow,
My legs plowed deeply through the crystal powder at my feet …
    HOW COULD THIS BE — so deep it lies — from storms few and discreet.

Yet, there it lay, a massive blanket built in silent haste,
    As week-by-week … yes, inch-by-inch … shrewd nature clothed this waste
That but a moment yesterday had seemed few tiny drifts;
    Yet truth lay bare — these eyes to stare — white snowflakes my mind sifts.

Great fortunes seldom grow through sterile ventures fraught with ease,
    But build through sweat and ceaseless pain 'midst rocks and churning seas.
The Caesars, Gettys, Hemingways with patience massed their sum,
    While massive oaks and awesome pines from tiny seeds did come.

Sinai, South Dakota. *Bit by bit the snow of winter accumulates to yield drifts deep and hard, showing the incredible power of persistence in making little things big and notable, through constant, diligent effort. Here the shadows of nearby trees have cast shadows upon the crystalline drifts that reach over the top of fences.*

Chapter 13 Respect

Respect

Earn respect through deeds renown,
    So all one's peers may place a crown
Upon your head in joyous pride ...
    Fresh youthful hope within reside.

Florence, Italy. *A painting of Napoleon Bonaparte I, Emperor of France for many years and general of the French army during the Napoleonic Wars, and great military and political leader in Europe, depicts a man of many talents whose crown was that of an earthly kingdom. Those intent on reaching much higher places search for a heavenly crown far beyond that sought by Napoleon.*

Hot Springs, South Dakota. *A bison cow protecting her calf is a formidable opponent for any predator intent on a meal. She will sacrifice all that she has, even her life, to defend the little one, and do so without a second thought.*

Fulfillment

Those striving to find happiness in this life will never obtain it.
    Only through selfless service to a fellow wayfarer through life
Can one receive the fulfillment deep within
    Which the inner being craves to satisfy,
Indeed was planted there by the Creator,
    That lusts for the eternal realm that propels one's deepest searching
For the reality of the unseen,
    That misty vision unfurled before the elect.

Sacrifice

Deep within the recesses of man's mind
    Lies a vast reservoir of desire
To sacrifice from the depths of self …
    To fulfill in selfless zeal
Beneficent goals far flung beyond man's realm.

Selfishness Defeated

First to serve himself, man's royal law proclaims,
    Relegating other fancies far from selfdom's aims,
Insuring that the self be primal surely can't be bad
    When if oneself should not be strengthened others might be sad,
Untended, duly crippled by a world of imperfection,
    Gleaning less of glory's stress from one's own desperation.

Serve the self indeed, we have no greater need,
    To be in health, of substance, wealth, that to our neighbor cede
Our very self, all that we have, to help him rise and stand,
    To lift him up, resigned of self, reaching forth one's hand.

Chapter 15

Self-Worth

Worth

Life is fraught with trialsome toil;
  We agonize about our worth.
Forever seems the pointless trial
  That troubles us who live on earth.

So seldom does one stop to see
  Our true identity in life,
Man's appointed destiny,
  His way caught up in Christ-like strife.

Yet therein lies our source of worth.
  We need not prove ourselves to be
Compared with other gents on earth,
  But to the One who set us free.

Worthiness

Haughty, uplifted eyes of man
  Cannot deliver love to yearning hearts,
Though titles and letters, accolades and resumes
  May lift his own ignoble vanity
To the mirage of worthiness.

Santiago, Chile. *While a male pea fowl displaying his feathers may not seem to be the most humble of all creatures, he nevertheless strives to display his worth as a potential mate and try to dazzle others. Might we strive to understand our own worth as well, not to dazzle but to serve?*

Chapter 16

Truth & Law

Truth

Truth shall always be victorious over lies and false witness,
  and in the course of time it shall be revealed,

That sweet victory of the Father's wisdom which prevails
  in the face of death and destruction,

Yes, even to the falling asunder of the gates of strong cities
  and marvelous bastions,

Reserved for the weak of heart and the failures of Satan's culture.

Florence, Italy. *This sculpture of David by Michelangelo is a remarkable work of art, one known throughout the world, but it is David's character that most impressed the Creator when He called this king of Israel a man after His own heart, a keeper of the Law, but not without his flaws and lapses.*

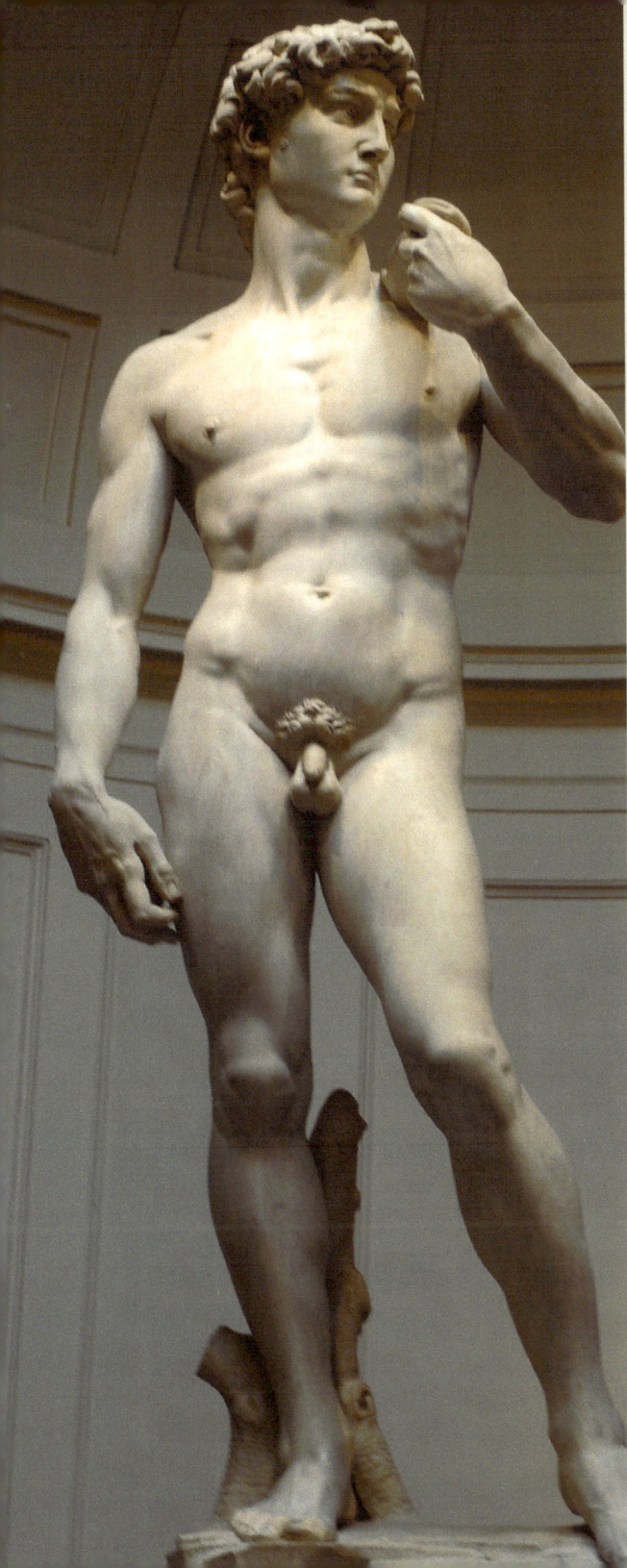

What Means the Law

Transgressing the law, in its infinite guises,
    Is such a vain error, it should not surprise us,
For what is it more then corrupting relations
    With men in God's image on sundry occasions.

The reason God gave it, without or within,
    (And hopefully in us, that we ought not sin)
Is so very simply to maximize joy,
    And peace, kindness, justice, and love which employ
The basis for living on God's firm foundation,
    To open broad vistas of liberty's nation.

Law poses no value except when it raises
    One's neighbor to copy God's infinite praises,
Resounding through heaven and earth with such vigor
    That David in Psalms could not stifle his rigor.

Wherein lies the wisdom to think, do, or say,
    Of soul, mind, and body through day's heated fray,
Except that one lift up one's brother, one's helm,
    To pleasures unending in God's wholesome realm.

And know we not Satan has planned pain and death,
    The opposite theory of God's righteous breath?

Endurance Through Trials

Afflicted

Afflicted and torn, the soldiers of truth,
    We wage royal battle 'gainst tyrants uncouth,
Those age-wicked phantoms that thrill to destroy
    Us scarred — yet resilient — contenders in joy,
Within heaven's mansions where lies ageless youth.

I cannot imagine a more troublous passion
    Than stirring the cauldron of Satan's dark chasm,
While thundering forth through my life simple faith,
    To topple strong kingdoms of vile greed and hate,
Through weakness and tears … a new world to fashion.

Affliction

Forget not the pain and suffering of days past,
    And be not overtaken with cares of this world.
Recall that affliction rests in the heart of the upright,
    And the righteous and wise reside in the house of sorrow.
Forget this not, my son; learn, and be wise.
    Listen to the admonition of your Creator.
Wear ornaments of white; avoid the darkness of ignorance.
    Face the truth of our own impotence,
And revel in the limitless joy of the One
    Who alone can place you within eternal habitations.
Fear not to hurt and suffer in this life,
    For after a little season you shall hurt no more,
But drink in of pleasures unending!

Casa Grande, Arizona. *A dust storm over the desert of Arizona inspires the idea of hardship within this present world, and endurance through the fierce winds and storms of life.*

Endurance Through Trials

Discouragement

Discouragement, that awful nemesis of human subsistence,
   Thrives desperately upon the austere plain of Satan's deception
Driving men to lethargy and despondency, to failure of goals
   and heartache among friends …
Yet cast out through relentless advance of the spirit,
   Accomplishment, moving ever forward despite the agonies
Of this world's sufferings, selfish zeal crucified daily!

Fruit from Grief

Firm, sweet fruit we bear, nutritious and tasty,
   When torturous winds of darkness threaten our very roots,
Whining gruesomely against creation's harmonious melodies
   Within spiritual harbors of safety… niches sheltering wild roses
Planted within deep soil, roots reaching out, drinking deeply
   Of bubbling brooks, warblers and vireos praising life anew,
Where lush leaves of green, skies of azure blue — Eden's paradise —
   Focus clearly the sufferings cast upon our servile flesh.
We lie upon mats of green, faces cast down upon the ground,
   Drinking in of God's good earth, fragrant odors of ageless saints …
Seeds of new fruits planted to grow quietly, resolutely,
   From us as verdant blossoms flavoring all the earth
With heaven's humbled sons.

Sinai, South Dakota. *Caught in a quandary — to leave the safety of the downspout, or risk injury or death by bolting out and scurrying to its hole — a thirteen-striped gopher contemplates a trial it must endure in this unfriendly world where the consequences of an incorrect decision could prove fatal.*

17 Endurance Through Trials

Pain for a Season

The soldier of truth finds rests
    Only in interims between tests.
Whether his days be grief or joy
    His goal is never realized,
And bitter trials bar his way
    To joy complete …
The new world's stage yet unseen.

Pain and Weakness

I pause amidst the burning pain of body's weakness spent
    Upon this lowly child of clay resigned to death's descent,
For some dark day I shall go down amidst the soil of earth
    And there recline in peace to sleep away this cruel hurt.

It does the soul much good, indeed the course of life must show,
    That rather 'midst the throes of pain we ought much wisdom sow,
Than revel in the arms of mirth, forgetting life's grand meaning,
    A birth to grander schemes than these, transformed to pure light beaming.

Death Valley, California. *Many pioneers in the old West feared the risky trek across the burning sands of Death Valley, but endured the trials of heat and exhaustion using patience and wisdom to survive and live for another day.*

Sinai, South Dakota. *Horses can endure incredible cold and distress as long as they are acclimated to the conditions. The four horses here merely wait out the storm, and patiently look forward to the days ahead when grass will again cover the land that now is a blanket of white.*

The House of Sorrow

The lens of a tear allows us to view the world more clearly
    Than a thousand days of mirth.
Better to spend your days in the house of sorrow
    Than to pass your time in fields of frivolity,
Wherein kernels of wisdom are few.

To the Overcomer

The road looked impossible, rutted in mud;
    No human could sensibly duel this great flood. *Continued from page 71*

Endurance Through Trials

Continued from page 70

Night's darkness enshrouded the way 'midst cold rain,
  Beating upon his numb body in pain.

No short-cut there seemed, to the left or the right,
  Just one way to go, straight ahead through the night,
And since humbled spirits can ill stand to rest,
  He started on walking to face the strong test.

The rain beat upon him, it knew no relenting,
  As straining he peered on ahead eyes a-squinting;
The north wind's redoubt cast its icy breath teasing,
  The mud on his boots like lead weights never ceasing.

Then far up ahead … could it be a faint light?
  His heart raced in gladness despite the sore plight.
He could not be sure for the road wound its way
  Between oak and elm trees that in the wind sway.

He thought then to run, but feet dumbly refused,
  And onto his knees fell exhausted, confused.
He could not go on … why begin such a race?
  Why did he not read sensibility's face?

The thought caught him short … unexpected, sublime,
  At such a rare moment when fear obstructs time.
Then ever so slowly a smile crossed his lips;
  Since when does the visible govern our steps?

He thought of impossible things he had tried,
  Remembered close friends who had stumbled and died.
Now here he was freezing in night's stormy sea,
  And questioning whether he'd sensible be!   *Continued on page 72*

Continued from page 71

Then suddenly out of the black of night's lair
    A force came upon him he knew not was there;
It gently wiped all of the tears from his face,
    And told him to walk on, to regain the pace.

He could not remember from whence came the power
    To pick up his feet and continue that hour,
But onward he plunged toward the light that he saw
    Far on down the road through the icy storm's maw.

Amazing things happened once making the change
    To cast doubt behind him, its vice rearrange,
For soon rain desisted, the wind spent her sting,
    The road firmed as miles passed … mud ceased to cling.

It seemed not too long, though ten hours he trekked,
    Before morning's twilight the country bedecked,
And what a fine sight, unexpected he viewed,
    Lush fields and green valleys, all earth golden hued.

And there on ahead but a stone's throw away
    Lay his home and his family in joyous array.
However he got there he ne'er could envision,
    But knew he just had to though stormy night's mission.

It runs in the family, this will to succeed,
    To conquer strong hardship that souls might be freed.
We strive for the mastery against awesome odds,
    And laugh at the price … and rejoice in our God!

Trials

Unless some trial should plague you,
    Some pain beset your quest,
Your fruit will not be plenteous,
    Nor sweet its last behest.

Endurance Through Trials

Trials Unnumbered

Think as you might that you have won the fight of life,
 Her pleading letters to your winsome soul, caution rife,
So quickly turn again serenity and calm to yet another trial,
 In endless purifying flames your heart in self denial,
That during this short tenure in flesh your inheritance not defile.

Refinement Through Trials

Trials do the heart good, purifying the spoils of self-deceit and hedonism,
 For threat to life rears up the heart to golden deeds,
And fear of loss throws selfishness to the wind.
 Forgiveness reigns true, and losing life that others may find it
Drowns out the cries of that old man's remembrance,
 Leading forth to that resurging new man,
Ready and waiting for his new home.

Oh Fickle Day

Oh, fickle day, you shame my zeal,
 Depriving life of heartfelt weal,
Hurtling toward the great abyss
 My dreams of youthful joyous bliss;
For each day now lies meshed in trouble,
 Griefs unending, heartaches double,
Since my God has set me free
 That trials may reap eternity.

Tried

Tested and tried you are in deed,
 Especially with your weakest creed;
Yet charge ahead with heart-felt thrust,
 With God's full armor shielding us.

18 Wisdom & Understanding

Attending to Wisdom

Better it is to attend the house of grief —
    for there the wise assemble —
Than the house of mirth, wherein sit the light of heart and
    shallow of discernment …
For many have been the times that great knowledge
    has been imparted to this soul
While groveling in the midst of fire, hail, and windstorm,
    assaulted on every side by the princes of evil.
So my soul prefers the company of the poor in spirit,
    the suffering companions of this cosmos,
That my years may bring forth fruit in abundance, focused
    through lenses of tears,
And my heart may grow rich through the poverty of
    this world's wealth.

Wells of Wisdom

How very often when the strife
    Of life unveils its desperate wages
Do we, the saints of heaven's life,
    Drink deeply from the wells of sages.

Fairburn, South Dakota. *Standing starkly against a summer sunset, a windmill preaches wisdom to all that pass by: drink of the waters of life that I will give you in a dry and thirsty land, using the power of the wind — the spirit that flows across the land — to bring you to the beautiful source of all light.*

Chapter 18

Wisdom & Understanding

Words and Wisdom

Within the unjust world of values turned upside down,
  Of black called white, and white called black,
How hard it is for those intent on pleasing their Creator
  To find solace amongst such lawlessness,
Where those profuse of verbiage — quick to speak but slow to listen —
  Are lauded and praised … fools honoring fools …
While the wise in their reticence are scarcely able
  To squeeze a pearl in edgewise,
Valued gems so often lost among the plethora
  Of cheap verbiage blurring in its flurry,
The sharp edge of wisdom
  Lost within this world of confusion.
Hold on to wisdom, young man,
  And uphold the fortress of life with your legions!

Farson, Wyoming. *An owl stares silently in the cool of the morning, seeming to epitomize wisdom, as this nocturnal bird has been associated with in many cultures across the earth. That stolid, steady stare reminds us to face squarely our trials in life and overcome through the power of the Creator of all life.*

Conquering Fear & Guilt

Death of Fear

In every venture, every quest,
    Each choice word your dreams invest,
Pure love and sense as mentors aid,
    While fear — that beast — to death is laid.

Fear Be Gone!

Cast out fear, dear man of flesh,
    And little can you not subdue;
Reach forth boldly hands of strength,
    Hold not back objectives true.

The conscience cannot bear the pain
    Of long-forgotten plans once bright,
Lit by strong ambitions stowed
    Amongst the lonesome dreams of night.

Somewhere 'long the road get smitten
    Plenteous hopes once flaming high;
Oh, to let winds fan their embers
    Once more up to freedom's sky.

Onward, upward, lay the pathway
    Strewn with bones on every side,
Only I must stay this venture
    Flinching not when pain has cried.

Death, where is thy sting, young man,
    And whence does fear so lay,
As when in liberty God's hands
    In love design this day.

Zion National Park, Utah. *The fearsome heights of these towering, sheer but beautifully sculptured cliffs remind the explorer that doubts and fears can afflict you only if you allow them. Love conquers even the greatest of fears.*

Conquering Fear & Guilt

Fear Cast Out

The greatest way to cast out fear from daily toil and pain,
    Is place your trust and fear in God, for He your sins has slain.
Obey Him with your total heart, your soul and mind entwined
    Within His will, His character inside yourself enshrined
Amongst your thoughts, your words and deeds forever reaching forth
    The praise of Him to every being on earth's resplendent course.

The fear of pleasing men so often torments fragile worth,
    And yes, we know that love perfected casts out fearful hurt.
By acting the Creator's song our works are not our own;
    Assaults and blows upon ourselves are to His glory sown.
If harsh assaults upon God rest for good deeds that we do,
    Then how can fear reside within this vessel carved for two?

Fear Be Lost

Of all the vices men draw vision clear,
    None so often bends his mind as fear.
Served in awful terror, or mixed well
    With jealousy and pride, self's conjured hell;
Sad ignorance of culture's lies, rejection
    Of soul's exceeding worth, God's own reflection.

Sinai, South Dakota. *The beauty of a white wild poppy drenched in morning's dew shouts forth the antithesis of captivity to fear and guilt. Its vista is heaven-ward, and its message is implanted within the purpose of its parts: the reproduction of its kind in the image of God.*

19 Conquering Fear & Guilt

Fear

When years were less and childhood reigned,
    I lived in carefree life unstained,
With life each moment — creeks and fields —
    Instilling peace, fond hopes revealed.

But worlds of men, their systems gross,
    Soon thrust their ugly heads so close
To tender idealistic dreams,
    And muddied childhood's pristine streams.

Fear crept in, came while I slept,
    As teenage years (their secrets kept
From uninstructed, star-struck minds)
    Steamed on through vain tradition's blinds.

It crept in as a house cat creeps,
    But bit as lions (reason sleeps),
And nearly swept me from my feet …
    Yet, Someone caught me, One discreet.

He showed, as knowledge blossoms spread
    Their fragrant gifts far overhead,
That men are men, no more, no less,
    And fear of flesh yields great distress … *Continued on page 84*

Valley of Fire, Nevada. *Warped and twisted rock layers typify the warped character of today's world after its fall from perfection, but the fears and guilt that the institutions of this world foster can be conquered by the ever-powerful working of the spirit of the Eternal through which all things were created.*

19 Conquering Fear & Guilt

Continued from page 82

For fear, while planted deep within
    Man's mind so he might flee from sin,
In constant daylong portions deals
    A spirit which with heartache reels.

In constant fear of life's next morn,
    Rose grim destruction, pain that's born
On each day's missions … sore distress …
    Oh, must this be! May God confess?

Yes, it pleased God to ease my fate,
    And to His Temple congregate,
For fear of man, though thrust within
    A pliant mind through men and kin,

Need never hold a man for long
    Within its clutches mighty … strong …
Once God makes plain the error raw,
    "Fear not man, son; fear my Law."

And soon as this man did,
    The truth could not be hid;
I stretched my wings and soared …
    Life yielded rich reward.

And after months — yes, even years — I lived again.

Fear Removed

What wasted energy, we servants of our God,
　　Who worry, fret, and sweat, our feet so faithless shod,
When fear and hapless living ought to the pit be thrown,
　　An ageless peace ascending, a joy where tears were sown.

Tenacity of Childhood Guilt

Our guilt lies so deeply upon heads grown gray,
　　Youth's deeds grimly chastised in angry dismay.
Though not gravely wicked, these deeds the heart spurns,
　　And toward father's wisdom the inner soul yearns.

Today yet we reel 'neath tradition's bequest:
　　Scars deeply entrenched, crying madly for rest …
Expunged of dark, hidden, lost valleys of doom,
　　Guilt purged, peace restored … that joy's fields might yet bloom.

www.ingramcontent.com/pod-product-compliance
Lightning Source LLC
Chambersburg PA
CBHW042011090426
42811CB00015B/1618